Black Bear

REFLECTIONS

REFLECTIONS *of the* WILDERNESS SERIES

by

KEN L. JENKINS

ICS BOOKS, INC.
Merrillville, Indiana

Dedication

This book is dedicated to my grandmother. Throughout my life she encouraged me and supported me and most of all listened to me. It has been that stability that has allowed me to pursue my goals.

Black Bear Reflections

Copyright © 1995 by Ken L. Jenkins

10 9 8 7 6 5 4 3 2 1

Printed in Singapore

Published by:
ICS Books, Inc.
1370 E. 86th Place
Merrillville, IN 46410
800-541-7323

Library of Congress Cataloging-in-Publication Data

Jenkins, Ken L.
      Black bear reflections / Ken L. Jenkins.
          p.   cm. — (Reflections of the wilderness series)
      ISBN 1-57034-013-7
      1. Black bear. 2. Black bear—pictorial works. I. Title. II. Series.
QL737.C27J435 1995
599.74'446—dc20   95-5103
                                         CIP

Table of Contents

Acknowledgments

Most everything that has been written about black bears has been based in part or in whole on the research and writing of Dr. Michael Pelton of the University of Tennessee. I know Mike for more than the world authority on black bears that he is. I sincerely thank him for his unselfish sharing of time, knowledge, and friendship and for his many years of dedication to the betterment of black bear populations across North America.

Preface

As far back as I can remember, my dad was taking me into the mountains, hiking, camping, and fishing. Black bears were always present along the roads, but to meet a bear in the backcountry was the most exciting experience of my younger years. Scouting allowed me to spend extended periods of time on outdoor projects and I can vividly remember the night that I camped in the Great Smoky Mountains and a large bear tripped over the guy lines on my tent and later crushed our icebox. Somehow, I only developed a deeper fascination with this "bruin of the shadows." I read every story on bears that I could find and spent several nights tossing in my nightmares after falling asleep with an *Outdoor Life* bear tale by Ben East and others. By the time I reached my teens, I was backpacking alone and spending much time wildlife watching. I developed a great respect for bears and became aware of their intelligence as a result of hours of observation and interaction. Through the years I have spent more time with bears than all other mammals and have photographed more bears than all other animals combined. My love for bears has grown, though I have yet to meet "Yogi" and have never considered myself "Grizzly Adams." Black bears are significant in indicating healthy wilderness and I want to spend as much time as possible in black bear country. I have had many great experiences involving bears and some of my favorite moments are reflected on the following pages.

The bear tramps over all, though few travelers have the pleasure of seeing him. On he fares through majestic forests and canyons, facing all sorts of weather, rejoicing in his strength, everywhere he is at home, harmonizing with trees and rocks . . . A happy fellow! His lines have fallen in pleasant places—lily gardens in silver-fir forests, miles of bushes in endless variety and exuberance of bloom over hill-waves and valleys and along banks of streams, canyons full of music and waterfalls, parks fair as Eden-places in which one might expect to meet angels rather than bears.

—John Muir, 1892, from *Muir Among the Animals*,1986, Sierra Club Books

Introduction

It had stormed throughout the night and after securing all my gear, I had fallen into a deep sleep as a result of the long hike and the peaceful sound of rain against the tent. The first rays of light were breaking through the trees as golden shafts through foggy woodlands. The smells of the woods were heavy and it seemed all right just to relax a bit longer in the comfort of my sleeping bag. Then came the sniffing sound at the base of my tent. There was no doubt in my mind what produced such a snort. My first look was not just out but up in the tree to see that my pack was still intact as it hung from an extended limb. Next, I pulled myself out of the tent to find my woolly visitor patrolling my fire ring with two fluffy cubs not far behind.

The fact that I had kept a clean camp allowed the bear family to pass along the trail to the nearby stream and allowed me to pick up my binoculars and my camera gear. The sow put the two cubs in the tree with a "woof" and proceeded to munch on the tender grasses along the bank. She knew that I was nearby and I knew not to crowd her nor to disturb her babies. It has always been this way when I have been fortunate enough to share the private lives of animals. There is a mutual respect that allows me to be a part of their world on their terms rather than mine. Nothing could have been more rewarding as time passed along this rolling stream and the mother bear coaxed her young down from the treetop and rolled back against the trunk to nurse her offspring.

Muir said that bears live in the most beautiful places in the world and I have certainly found that to be true. Some of the most wonderful days of my life have been spent in the presence of bears.

There was a time when black bears were more abundant throughout Canada, the United States, and Mexico. In recent years many changes have occurred in the black bear's habitat and he is still adapting and holding on in areas where he receives help from authorities. A male bear can weigh 250 to 400 pounds and be four and a half to six feet in length, however, record males have reached nine feet in length and have weighed up to six hundred pounds. Their foods vary from leaves and sedges to berries, insects, and nuts. More needs to be understood about the black bear but writings of outdoorsmen as far back as William Bartram in 1791 suggest that the bear is no threat to humans. He writes, "Bears are numerous, strong creatures and prey on the fruits of the country. . . . I never could learn a well-attested instance of their attacking mankind."

CHAPTER ONE

Spring Awakening

When the new leaves of spring unfold and days begin to lengthen, I feel it my duty to trek into the forest and check on my favorite mammal, the black bear. Cubs are born in the den during January and February and it isn't unusual to find the bears moving out of the den by March. But for me, May is the best time to invest many mornings afield bear watching.

Timing is everything in approaching bears. This tree is located along a drainage where the bears can come in undetected. In spring they seem to favor ash and chestnut oak leaves. After watching for an hour or so, it is clear that this is a sow and two yearling cubs. The bears used two styles of climbing: the sow held the tree with strong forepaws and pushed with her hindquarters while at least one of the yearlings used a "walking-up-the-tree" type of motion. An old saying in the mountains is that "a bear can climb a tree faster than a man can fall out of one." After hours of moving up and down these trees the three slept until it was too dark for my observation.

After returning to the valley many evenings, the bear's tolerance of me began to grow and I cautiously located myself closer to the stand of trees. The sow always left the cubs in nearby woods as she came to feed on these choice leaves. She came in with her nose in the air in order to determine exactly where I was. As she moved to the tree and looked back over her shoulder, she grunted only once as she climbed thirty feet or more to feed. (The balance that bears have is amazing as they stretch for a limb while standing on a swaying branch that seems much too weak to support them.)

4

(*left*) Walking back from the grove my mind was tuned into bear facts. The whitetails were dropping fawns yet the newborns were so perfectly camouflaged it would be rare for a bear to find them. The doe had licked all scent from her young at birth and this fawn instinctively remained motionless.

(*below*) In eastern woodlands, squawroot is a much-sought-after food for bears in early spring. After their system shuts down in winter this is most likely a laxative. Surely this clump will disappear overnight as the bears retrace the same trails back through the forest.

GREAT SMOKY MOUNTAINS NATIONAL PARK, TENNESSEE & NORTH CAROLINA

There is no easy way to follow a bear. They tend to take the shortest route from point A to point B and that route may be straight up a ridge and is always through an almost impenetrable stand of vegetation. From the Smokies in Tennessee to the Olympics in Washington to the Canadian Rockies of Alberta, black bears have shaken me off their trail consistently by leading me into the roughest, thickest, most frustrating stretches of terrain imaginable. My instincts of late lead me to find signs that the bear was there and then to wait for them. If they do not show, I have invested in another exercise of patience. However, if my plan pays off, I will spend an extended amount of time watching a bear undisturbed. At the very least, I will observe several birds and possibly small mammals and will have added some quality to my life by just being out in nature.

(*above*) This fellow was a prime specimen and seemed proud of his condition. He braced himself between two limbs and violently shook the tree. Surely he did the tree a service, as much deadwood fell from the crown very near to where I was kneeling. The bears seem more relaxed when I remain in a lower position so I always approach from my knees and eventually sit. This male moved throughout the branches and came very close before heading to an opening in the forest.

(*right*) Tearing away at the bark of the tree the male made a complete circle while stripping the cambium layer. Often the tree will die from this type of affliction but it is early spring and these wounds should heal.

CHAPTER TWO

Caring for the Young

Only when the sow climbed the tree to feed did I realize how small her spring cub was. It is mid-March and food is scarce but the female bear strips the branches as the young cub sniffs each place she has gnawed. After a short time of feeding she will retreat to a private place and allow the cub to nurse. In the meantime, the tiny ball of fur is preoccupied with every bug on every branch. His sharp little claws hold tight to the trunk. When the mother bear continues to feed she seems to know just what is choice. She climbs a single tree and gorges herself on leaves near the top then climbs down, walks fifty feet to the next tree, and huffs up to the crown for another meal. Feeding in this manner is an adult practice and more often than not the tiny cub prefers to observe rather than to participate.

GREAT SMOKY MOUNTAINS NATIONAL PARK, TENNESSEE & NORTH CAROLINA

It was May and every morning for weeks I had followed this sow and her three spring cubs. Some mornings it took an hour or more to locate her but she was staying in the same general area. There was heavy brush and in some places high grasses and dense woodlands so sighting her was often difficult. A crack of a dead limb when she was feeding helped but mostly I found her when multiple ears poked up above the grasses to investigate my intrusion. Watching this bear family was a very personal activity for me. I was always alone and stayed at a distance once I spotted the bears. The sow had lost an eye sometime in her past and it seemed to me that she relied heavily on her sense of smell. It was always her choice to move closer to me to see what my intentions were. I could never say whether she knew any more about me than my scent but she definitely developed a tolerance for me, and my involvement in her daily routine seemed of less concern to her each visit.

It was early one Saturday morning when I noticed she was keeping the cubs very close and it was usually at this time that she crossed the creek and disappeared into heavy rhododendron growth for the afternoon. Instead she turned in my direction and slowly ambled within fifteen feet of where I sat. After a couple of

11

indirect glances, she rolled back in a very vulnerable position and took one cub under each forearm and began to feed them. This was the ultimate compliment, paid out of mutual respect. The sound was the very chorus of contentment. A magnified buzz, hum, and whine carried through the forest as each cub took turns filling himself. Except for a couple of clicks of my camera I did not move and only on two occasions did the mother bear look in my direction, though she was keenly aware of my position. Soon she rolled over and began to sleep with two of the three cubs just beside her.

The third cub insisted on climbing atop the female and biting her ears or "bopping" his siblings on the head. After making a couple of passes in front of his much larger mom, she placed her huge paw on top of him and his nap began immediately. Never to betray her trust I sank back on the damp forest floor hardly believing what I had been so privileged to witness. The nap lasted for almost an hour, at which time she moved through the stream and disappeared, off to her regular afternoon resting area.

CHAPTER THREE

The Importance of Climbing

(*left*) A woof or pop of jaw sends the cubs for a tree. Their second reaction is to look for the source of intrusion and then scamper on up the tree. These twins shared the tree trunk and progressed higher at the same speed.

(*right*) Cubs play-fight for position on favored tree limbs. Playing is an education for the young and, though more controlled in adults, it is very much a part of a bear's life. Many naturalist-writers have concluded that bears have a sense of humor.

This little fellow was very tangled up in grapevines that covered the tree trunk. The process of coming down appears much more difficult for the cub than going up. In this instance the mother bear had continued across a meadow, leaving the cub to fight his way out of his entanglement. After several attempts, he began to bawl and only then did the sow stand to investigate his alarm. Without intervening she took steps toward the tree then departed. This seemed encouragement enough for the small bruin. He tore away at the vines and popped out at the base of the tree. When he bounced through the meadow the female waited and rewarded him for his efforts with a couple of licks on the head.

Climbing and play seem to go hand in hand for the cubs and though they may be forty feet or more in a tree, I have seen only two cubs fall. On both occasions the height was around twenty feet and both times a sibling had pushed the second cub off the limb. The fallen youngster did no more than grunt and race back up the tree for a second bout.

CHAPTER FOUR

The Displaced Yearling

In heavy forests in several parts of the country, I encounter the displaced "yearling" bear. Born in winter, inseparable from his mother the following spring, summer, and fall, the cub has spent a second winter with the female and her cubs. This spring he was a bit more curious and tended to wander farther from the safety of his family. He was not prepared, however, for the abrupt scolding that he received when his mother decided to wean him. Several chases up the ridge and an occasional swat persuaded him to keep his distance and eventually to seek out a home of his own. The female would go into her mating cycle once more. The bond is somewhat severed but never entirely broken as there seems to be a lifelong connection with mother and home territory.

18

(*above*) A lonesome yearling carries a pelvic bone found in the meadow. For days he defended his "bone" against bee and butterfly. Possibly this was his "security blanket" in the absence of his mom.

(*right*) The frustration of being bored and alone is best handled by long naps, according to this yearling black bear. Adjusting takes time and the transition between having mom near and striking out on his own seems to be a tough one for most youngsters.

CHAPTER FIVE

Bears along the Trail

(*above*) Rocky Mountain habitat produces beautiful black bears. This view is Kootenay Provincial Park in Jasper, Alberta. On a very cold September morning I climbed to a rockslide just below this aspen grove.

(*inset*) Climbing through lush forests I heard brush moving just off trail. My eye caught a movement and out of the green came a very healthy pine marten. His surprise was greater than mine and he quickly disappeared in the same direction.

21

In the Kootenay area I spotted this large male bear. Rather, I should say that he spotted me because as I walked he charged across the trail in front of me and quickly climbed a bare slope. I watched through binoculars as he moved higher, investigating cracks in the rocks as he went. To the left I saw a small band of bighorn sheep moving left to right down the steep ridge. The bear immediately sensed the sheep and sat down. The sheep moved all around him within thirty yards. There was never a sign of aggression on the bear's part nor was there panic among the sheep. The flock passed and the bear got up and ambled down the ridge in my direction. More than an hour later I located him snoozing away on a large boulder. Surely he was "counting sheep" in his dreams. My only conclusion was that the number of animals prevented him from considering them a meal. The safety-in-numbers rule allowed the sheep to graze and proceed along the slope. It was another lesson in nature's classroom.

It was in Kings Canyon National Park that I first observed the brown phase of the American black bear. Since boyhood I have read the journals of John Muir regarding this fascinating region in the Sierras of California. Muir had developed a fondness for the bear and his role in nature. As I hiked through the giant sequoias and thought of Muir's early adventures, I scanned the rockslides for pika or puma. Late in the day as I returned through the canyon, I spotted a large bear in low light and tall grasses. As I moved closer, I was shocked by the size and color of this cinnamon-shaded beauty. The bear popped his jaw twice, which let me know he was uncomfortable with my approach, so I moved back to the trail toward camp.

The typical black coloration is most dominant especially in the eastern half of the continent.

KINGS CANYON NATIONAL PARK, CALIFORNIA

The brown or cinnamon phase of the black bear is often confusing in areas where grizzlies share the same habitat.

24

For lovers of the outdoors, walking along the trail is like entering a residential area. To know that beneath every boulder, every fallen log, and inside every hollow tree there lives another creature, adds great meaning to a walk in the woods. The black bear's presence in our forests indicates a healthy balance in nature. Often the signs that bears leave behind are our only evidence of them. A truly wild bear is elusive and prefers his solitude. Walking this trail in the forest I heard an instant crashing through the underbrush. A young black bear had caught my scent as I rounded the bend and was now at full throttle toward the closest tree.

After climbing several feet, the young black bear paused and peeked around the tree trunk to see if I had pursued him. If a bear can run up to thirty miles per hour in short bursts, then he surely climbs at half that speed. The movement of this bear up the tree was swift and after he paused, he proceeded to reach the crown of the tree, where he eventually went to sleep.

This hollow log in a poplar tree had been used the past winter as a den. While a bear den can be anything from a depression in the ground to a well-excavated cave under a rocky ledge, the majority of dens in the Appalachians are blown-out trees. The tree may have been struck by lightning or just torn out by the wind, but in any case, the black bear enjoys the cavity high in the tree and will sleep in a very contorted position for weeks at a time.

A subadult bear retreats down the trail near dusk only to stand and look back over his shoulder. Many naturalists have found the actions and characteristics of the black bear quite humanlike.

Signs of bear activity along the trail are evidence of the bear's diet. A fresh dig may be where a bear has dug for roots or possibly for the larvae in a wasp nest. A torn log is probably where the bear has found termites or grubs of some sort.

MOUNT RANIER NATIONAL PARK, WASHINGTON

Even the track of the black bear resembles a human track. Hiking in wilderness areas becomes greatly enhanced when the hiker starts to see bear tracks in the trail ahead. Bears frequently use "people trails" and oftentimes hiking trails have been built along game trails. Bears encountered along the trail are quick to find cover and if the bear is coming in your direction, he is probably looking for a place to get off the path.

Deep in the forest where bears spend much of their lives many other mammals also thrive. In most of the black bears' range across North America deer coexist in great numbers. Although there have been reports that a bear has taken a fawn, most cases involved a deer that was sick or injured. These whitetail fawns are alert to every smell and sound and can quickly disappear from any would-be predator.

In all my years of "living" in the backcountry of America, I have never felt truly threatened by a black bear. Theodore Roosevelt wrote in his journal around 1893, ". . . a black bear is not usually a formidable opponent, and though he will sometimes charge, he is much more apt to bluster and bully than to come to close quarters." In areas where picnickers have left scraps, bears, being opportunists, have turned to panhandling. Feeding a bear represents misguided kindness—not to mention, it is an illegal and dangerous practice. Fed bears quickly lose their fear of humans and approach for reasons of expecting food. In most every case the bear loses, a result of becoming vulnerable in that new area or killed as he attempts to return "home."

Among my favorite naturalist writers of all time is Sally Carrighar, whose writings in the thirties and forties were based entirely on her personal observations. Often she wrote from the animal's perspective. Her book *One Day at Beetle Rock* contains an informative and fascinating chapter on the American black bear. Recently, as I sat on Beetle Rock in California's Sequoia National Park, where bears still roam in decent numbers, I recalled her account of a female bear nursing her young: "She had dropped back into a sitting position and held her forepaws aside. The two bounded forward, climbed onto her legs, and pressed against her body, their ears level with her shoulders. She drew them closer with her forepaws on the fur of their hips. . . . With the first mouthful of milk the cubs started a small, weird hum, which grew louder as their stomachs filled." Sally Carrighar's book *One Day at Beetle Rock* was written in 1943 and has been republished by Bison Books, University of Nebraska, Lincoln.

32

All wild animals have an invisible circle that when crossed will prompt them to flee or fight. I encountered this bear on a windy day in very thick grasses. He has his ears forward, his hair is up on his back, and he is popping his jaws. All of the aforementioned are signs of discontent that will lead to a quick retreat or possibly a charge of some order. Fortunately, the former was true in the case of the bear pictured. Each year I witness dozens of visitors to natural areas as they directly approach bears for a multitude of reasons, including "just to see how close I could get." Bears are for the most part better behaved than people, though the log books in many parks show instances of bites and scratches due to aggressive behavior.

Above, a wet mother bear tries to escape the heat and the aggravation of her year-ling cub. The young bear insists on being as close as possible to the sow so her only recourse is to fall asleep and completely ignore him. If the message were disregarded she would normally scold him with a growl or relocate him with a swat.

The message soon becomes clear to the young bear as the mother drifts off into a deep afternoon nap. The next best thing to being beside mom is to be just above her so the yearling picks out a choice limb and mimics his mom's behavior.

A rhododendron slick is an almost impenetrable type of vegetation to man and most other large mammals. The black bear, however, finds this type of terrain quite an acceptable refuge. Whether a daybed or a winter denning site, the thickly matted vegetation provides shelter and uninterrupted territory in which to retire.

When disturbed, a female bear moves to a higher ridge to oversee her surroundings and possibly to catch a better scent of the intruder. Meanwhile, the spring cub stays pressed close to his mother until she signals that everything is safe again.

A swamp such as the one above provides good habitat for bears. Ample food, shelter, and water allows the bears to thrive in this type of environment. Many other mammals share a swampy home with the black bear. His cousin the raccoon usually exists in large numbers as well as opossum and squirrel. The otter (pictured right) is especially well adapted to this watery terrain and accepts the bear as no threat or concern.

Above, a sow and cub pause beside a mountain stream. The female lifts her forepaw on the tree trunk to cool her underside in the summer heat. Vegetation on the shore provides food for the sow and shelter for the cub should the mother bear wander away. Oftentimes the bears will cross back and forth in the stream. The cub may initially protest but if need be the sow will take her nose and push him into the water knowing that he can swim to safety.

An adult bear uses the water to cool itself and possibly to find relief from insects. This bear waded and swam the river for about a quarter mile before coming to a sandy spot where he napped for a long while. Bears are creatures of habit and often use the same paths, even stepping in the same tracks. Perhaps this swimming hole is used often by this and other bears.

CHAPTER SIX

Autumn's Golden Harvest

Autumn is a crucial period in the black bear's life. He must find ample quantities of food in order to produce the necessary fat surplus to endure the winter. I have observed "years of plenty" where falling acorns fell like rain in deciduous woodlands and hickory nuts were also in abundant supply. In these years the bears gorge themselves and it seems that more cubs emerge from the den the following spring. A fruitful autumn means that bears are not wandering out of natural areas and are thus made safer by lack of need to search out foods. Every animal in the forest thrives in these times.

In contrast, I have witnessed late spring freezes that nipped the buds on the oak and hickory trees causing a near total failure during the fall harvest. The bears become stressed and lean and search extensively for any sort of food. This search takes them into rural areas and across major thoroughfares where roadkills occur and poachers prey on their predicament. Spring arrives quietly and few cubs bounce along behind the sows that survived the winter.

The autumn search for food continues to direct the movement of the bears. Daybeds are often scooped out in oak groves where food is plentiful and time can be spent resting and feeding. The bears munch acorns by the hundreds, finding them by sight and smell amidst newly fallen leaves.

Autumn is truly a beautiful time when wildlife species are observed in prime condition. This adult male bear is fattened and appears ready to endure even the harshest
of winters. Having eaten the proper foods, he has a sleek coat and keen senses.

The woodlands and all their inhabitants peak at nearly the same time. The bears will wander along the same trails daily as they pass into areas of abundant food supply.

(*right*) As this bear reaches to mark the tree, much is still not understood about this practice. Although it is said that the bear is marking territory, research shows that territories overlap and marks go unnoticed by other bears. I have witnessed bears investigating the claw marks of another bear with little more than a sniff and no obvious concern for leaving the area.

Bears do seem to enjoy rubbing trees. This exercise seems to relieve itching while removing dead hair. When a vigorous rub is complete it has been my good fortune to witness a bear locating a small bush or tree and crouching over it to complete the rub on his underside.

Though chiefly nocturnal, the raccoon is often observed feeding within the same grove as the black bear during autumn. His means of escape is similar, though he can obviously disappear into smaller cavities in the ground or a tree. The raccoon eats most anything available and often dunks his food in water to aid digestion. This raccoon and three others occupied the same small stretch of woodlands where a large male bear fed constantly.

By the time harvests are available in the forests, the high country is being coated by late autumn snowfall. The bears are aware of the short time of feasting and will feed day and night to acquire the layer of fat that insulates them in winter.

CHAPTER SEVEN

The Spirit of Wildness

Meet Number 75, as this bear came to be known. I spent many sunny afternoons with this bear in the Great Smoky Mountains National Park of Tennessee. The bear was a big male for this part of the country. He seemed well behaved and well adapted to his range. One evening in passing through an area of the park that con-

tains an active grist mill, this old fellow gave in to temptation and went through the wall of the mill to inspect a curious scent. He was likely attracted to the tallow on the old mill wheel.

Resource management realized that this behavior could not be tolerated and that this bear would likely repeat his unbearlike act, so they tranquilized him and tagged his ear Number 75. Number 75 was then moved to a remote area of the park several miles from the mill. Bears have an excellent homing ability, especially adult bears. It could be said that they have superb topographical observation when released in territories that they have never seen. In addition, they are very habituated to their home range and once reaching that range can zero in on most any section they choose. And so was the case for this bear, for in a few days he showed up at the mill. He was moved again farther away, out of state, and more

GREAT SMOKY MOUNTAINS NATIONAL PARK, TENNESSEE & NORTH CAROLINA

than a hundred miles up the Appalachian chain near Roanoke, Virginia.

In a couple of weeks, ole Number 75 was reported to have been seen about sixty miles northeast of the Smokies. The newspaper outdoor correspondent picked up on the story to say, "There is just one place on earth that Number 75 wants to live and it is the Great Smoky Mountains National Park and he's headed home!"

Authorities knew that this bear would be better off living in a natural area where he was not tempted by this irresistible urge. He was moved up on the Blue Ridge Parkway where the next day he was poached and found near the roadside. A terrible end for such a noble bear.

Even the loss of one bear due to unnatural causes is of concern to all true outdoors-men. As rural America slowly disappears the black bear has learned many ways to adapt to living near humans. In other ways his needs are ignored as he struggles to hold on in an ever-changing world.

As autumn foods are consumed and fat is accumulated, the biological clock begins to tell the bear that it is denning time. Bears are seen napping more often throughout the day. The sows with cubs will den first, followed by the males. It is said that an orphaned cub cannot find a den without the instincts of his mom but there is much documentation showing that orphaned cubs have survived winters alone.

By December most colder climates have a covering of snow and the bears are tucked away in their dens. In areas of milder temperatures, the denning process cannot be described as a true hibernation as bears rouse on occasion and move through the woods. Their digestive system does, however, shut down and their intestine becomes knotted with tissue. Thus they neither feed nor pass any waste. Their dens are clean and with all necessary preparation during fall the bear will expel a winter's worth of waste in spring and emerge for another eventful season.

There could never be enough shared about the experiences that man has had with black bears. From sportsman to naturalist to wildlife biologist, journals are filled with colorful accounts of men and women spending time in bear country and coming away impressed and enriched.

The great naturalist Henry David Thoreau wrote in his journal on February 18, 1860, "I think that the most important requisite in describing an animal is to be sure and give its character and spirit, for in that you have, without error, the sum and effect of all its parts, known and unknown. Surely the most important part of an animal is its anima, its vital spirit, on which is based its character and all the peculiarities by which it most concerns us."

Though volumes have been written and much needs to be understood, the character and spirit of the black bear dwell among all who love these great lands. An animal is as much a part of our past as it should be of our future. Studies are under way to try and understand how the bear can sleep in such a contorted position with no skeletal or muscular breakdown. If a medicine could be developed synthetically to duplicate this enzyme in the bear, perhaps crippling diseases such as osteoporosis could be treated. The world of wildlife has much to give. May we always learn from it.

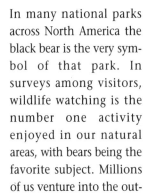

In many national parks across North America the black bear is the very symbol of that park. In surveys among visitors, wildlife watching is the number one activity enjoyed in our natural areas, with bears being the favorite subject. Millions of us venture into the outdoors each year. As habitat shrinks for the black bear we are no longer just observers but participants in the life and future of the bears. There is no greater satisfaction than to know that you spent time with a wildlife subject in its natural behavior and left it undisturbed.